ENJOYING GOD'S GRACE

Enjoying God's Grace

TERRY VIRGO

KINGSWAY PUBLICATIONS
EASTBOURNE

First published in 1989 by Frontier Publishing
This edition 1999

ISBN 0 85476 841 6

Published by:
KINGSWAY PUBLICATIONS
Lottbridge Drove, Eastbourne, E. Sussex, BN23 6NT.

Cover design by Pinnacle Creative

Designed and produced for the publishers by
Bookprint Creative Services,
P.O. Box 827, BN21 3YJ, England.
Printed in Great Britain.

Thank You To . . .

Mary Austin for all her hard work in listening to recordings of my preaching on this theme and for working through my notes in order to present this book to you in its present form.

Contents

Preface

This book has been published with a definite purpose in view. It is suitable either for house-groups or individuals who want to study a particular Bible theme in a practical way. The goal is not simply to look up verses and fill up pages of a notebook, but to fill in gaps in our lives and so increase our fruitfulness and our knowledge of God.

Both of Peter's letters were written to 'stimulate . . . wholesome thinking' (2 Peter 3:1). He required his readers to think as well as read! We hope the interactive approach of this book will have the same effect. Stop, think, apply and act are key words.

If you are using the book on your own, we suggest you work through the chapters systematically, Bible and notebook at your side and pen in hand. If you are doing it as a group activity, it is probably best to do all the initial reading and task work before the group sessions – this gives more time for discussion on key issues which may be raised.

Unless otherwise stated, all quotations from the Bible are from the New International Version.

Terry Virgo

Introduction

When Charles Wesley experienced the grace of God, he couldn't keep it to himself! The discovery was too glorious to imagine and too wonderful to hold back, so he wrote:

> Oh, that the world might taste and see
> The riches of His grace!
> The arms of love that compass me
> Would all mankind embrace.

For many of us, such excitement over the grace of God is puzzling. We can remember the joy and release we experienced when we were born again, but now our Christian life has settled down and we have lost much of our enthusiasm for God's grace. 'I've received his saving grace,' we say to ourselves, 'and I want people to put their trust in God. But I don't know anything about the riches of his grace. What are the riches of God's grace anyway? Am I missing out on something?'

Sadly many believers are missing out but they do

not realise it, because they have never heard about the depth of God's grace and how it affects them. They live apparently normal Christian lives, but secretly they feel that they are fighting a losing battle. If they were honest, they would admit that they are often bored with their Christianity. God's grace, his free undeserved favour, was exciting once, but now . . . well, now life is almost mundane and grace applies only to those who have not yet trusted Christ to save them.

Many believers live under the shadow of condemnation and therefore have little to rejoice about. They allow themselves to be governed by their feelings, which they occasionally try to overcome by willpower. Since their minds play an insignificant role in their Christian lives, their emotions and their willpower are left to battle it out between them.

This state of affairs is particularly sad in the light of Jesus' words, 'You will know the truth, and the truth will set you free' (no reference to emotions or willpower here!). When we understand the truth, we are released – especially when the truth tells us that God loves us unconditionally. He has loved us with an everlasting love and always will do. He has made us totally and eternally righteous in his sight through our faith alone.

The truth is almost too good to be true! God's grace is so amazing that Christian teachers are often too nervous to declare it fully. They fear that if believers really grasp how freely God loves them, they will live carelessly and take advantage of that grace. To prevent this happening, these teachers make sure that they add a number of provisos to the message of grace – an action which actually has the effect of obscuring its transforming power.

There is a very real danger in the message of 'free grace'. It could lead to irresponsible and even sinful living. Peter addresses that fact when he says, 'Live as free men, but do not use your freedom as a cover-up for evil' (1 Peter 2:16). But if we add the warnings too quickly, we shall muffle the sound of the good news and blunt the edge of its power to deliver.

When I was at school I used to paint watercolour landscapes. Once I had painted a blue sky, I could not paint a green tree against that sky until the blue paint had dried. I knew that if I attempted to add the tree too soon, the colours would run into one another. Either I waited patiently until the blue had dried, or I totally ruined the picture!

Many Christians are too quick to add disciplines to the message of grace. Before new believers have ever understood that God loves them unconditionally, they add, 'But of course, you must always . . . and you ought never to . . .' The result is often that Christians simply believe that God loves them if they are good. We are back to salvation by works, not salvation that works.

This is not to say that Christian discipline is unimportant. On the contrary, the apostle Paul, who decries every hint of legalism, also calls us to godly discipline – a discipline which is not based on the legalistic hopeful search to earn God's blessing, but on the faith that what God says is true of us.

We work things out because we believe God is at work in us. As Peter says, we are to 'make every effort', not in a vain attempt to get through against overwhelming odds, but because we have been given 'everything we need for life and godliness' (2 Peter 1:3). We make the effort because we are motivated by a deep conviction that God is for us and with us. Our work is the product of faith and springs from the life within.

Godly discipline is not a work of legalism but a work of faith. The acid test is therefore: do I discipline myself because I've got to win God's favour or because I want to enjoy God's grace? The discipline of faith looks fully at what God says is already true and gladly lives in the light of it.

We must follow Paul's example. Though he formerly persecuted the church of God, he received and gloried in the free grace of God, declaring, 'By the grace of God I am what I am, and his grace to me was not without effect. No, I worked harder than all of them – yet not I, but the grace of God that was with me' (1 Corinthians 15:10). Clearly, there is no tinge of legalism in all his hard work.

My prayer is that as you study *Enjoying God's Grace*, God will grant you a richer enjoyment of the fullness of his salvation. May it be a life transforming experience for you! May God reveal the truth about his grace to you and set you free to enter into a brand new relationship with him!

Terry Virgo

1

Reigning in Life

John sits in the packed conference hall and listens intently to the speaker. 'We are more than conquerors through him who loved us,' the speaker exclaims enthusiastically. 'Thanks be to God who always leads us in triumphal procession in Christ! The Father has called us to reign in life – it's in his Word. Tremendous truths, aren't they?'

All around the hall people nod and verbalise their agreement: 'Amen', 'Praise you, Lord', 'Hallelujah'. But John sits quietly and thinks hard.

'I'm supposed to be a conqueror,' he says to himself sadly. 'So why do circumstances always seem to be on top of me? Why do I feel I'm only just coping? Why am I such a loser? Why don't I experience complete victory over temptation, sin and condemnation? Why do I always seem to be letting God down?' To John, the idea of 'reigning in life' is like a far off mountain peak – beautiful but totally unattainable.

Pull up your socks

He returns home feeling condemned but convinced that if the Bible says he is a winner, then it's time he started winning. 'To begin with, I'll write down all the things I should be doing,' he says to himself.

- What sort of things would you expect to see on his list?

After about a week of 'successful reigning' John oversleeps and misses his prayer time. The following morning, he has to read two portions of Scripture in his daily notes. This means that he doesn't have time to pray for as many people as he had planned. He feels guilty about this but can't do anything except perhaps catch up later in the evening. By the end of about three weeks, he is six days behind on the notes, has twenty-seven people he has not regularly prayed for and has virtually given up on the whole reigning process!

Six months later John hears another preacher. 'We reign in life!' he declares enthusiastically. John immediately feels very guilty and thoroughly wretched for having allowed himself to succumb to the temptation to 'stop reigning'. Full of remorse, he goes home and reinstates the original spiritual targets. Then he plunges himself into fervent activities by which he hopes to rid himself of the guilt associated with not trying hard enough. 'I wonder how long I can reign this time?' he asks himself as he wearily glances over the nine

chapters of Leviticus he has got to read before
7.00 a.m.

Although the concept is scriptural, being a
winner would appear to be a day-to-day impossibility. The well-intentioned Christian is crippled by
the activities he feels he needs to perform in order
to be victorious. As time passes, the pattern of up
and down spiritual behaviour becomes familiar to
him. Indeed, he comes to expect it. And he feels
more like a miserable slave condemned to endure a
long slow death than a joyful son and heir reigning
triumphantly in eternal life.

• If John came to you, what would you say to him?

Justified by evangelical laws?

The 'striving to please God' story strikes a chord
in most of our hearts. Time and time again we
have resolved to try harder at reigning but have
ended up tired, depressed and resigned to failure.
Why?

Have you ever wondered whether 'striving to
please God' is the way to 'reign in life'? Most of us
never question it. We have, rather, been taught from
the early days of our Christian life that prayer, Bible
study, fellowship and evangelism are 'what you
ought to do if you want to be right with God'. So we
doggedly plough on through all the things we
ought to do, believing that God will smile when
we are faithful and frown when we are not.

We assume, therefore, that once we have received

salvation as a free gift, we then reign by working hard at the 'evangelical laws'. After all, how else could we reign?

• Read Galatians 3:2, 3; 4:10, 21.

The Galatians had been justified by faith and now they were trying to reign by observing the requirements of the law. No wonder the apostle Paul was indignant! 'You foolish Galatians!' (Galatians 3:1) he chided them. He recognised that they were not just developing a slightly different emphasis but were actually turning to a different gospel (Galatians 1:6).

Old Covenant versus New Covenant

Legalistic obedience to laws which Christians have invented such as 'Don't handle, don't taste, don't touch' may sound good, but Paul says that they are useless (Colossians 2:20–23). This is an Old Testament method of living a New Testament life. And it fails every time because, like oil and water, you cannot mix them together. They are entirely different Covenants which have a drastically different effect on people.

The Old Covenant was given to Moses who, on returning from Mount Sinai to the valley, found the Israelites worshipping the golden calf. In anger, he broke the tablets on which the Ten Commandments had been written and ordered the Levites to execute judgement on the people.

- What happened? (Exodus 32:28)

The New Covenant was given to the disciples through the Holy Spirit at Pentecost. When Peter descended from the upper room, he accused the people of an infinitely worse crime than idolatry. They had killed God's Son, the Lord of glory. Surely the penalty for this wicked act should be severe.

- What happened? (Acts 2:41)

The two Covenants are totally different. The Old Covenant was written on stone (Exodus 31:18), the New Covenant is inscribed on hearts (Hebrews 8:10). The Old emphasised obedience to law and brought judgement and condemnation. The New focuses on the free gift of grace and brings mercy and release.

Before Jesus died we were judged by the law but when we trusted Christ to save us, we relied on him to fulfil the law for us and to set us free from its demands. Thus:

Christ is the end of the law ... for everyone who believes (Romans 10:4).

- Look up 2 Corinthians 3:9 and note:

- What the Old Covenant is called.

- What the New Covenant is called.

- The Old Covenant is now – what? (Hebrews 8:13)

Reigning in life

When God gives something new, it has no hint of oldness about it. The first miracle Jesus performed was to turn ceremonial cleansing water into wine (John 2:1–11). In other words, he took something relating to law and gave it a totally new flavour! Following his Pentecost experience, Peter offered the people not another set of laws but a new experience of the power of the Holy Spirit (Acts 2:17).

The old has gone, the new has come! (2 Corinthians 5:17)

Christians are not patched up creations but new ones! God has given us a completely new life. We are no longer saved by obeying external laws; godly desires are now written on our hearts (2 Corinthians 3:2,3) and new life comes flooding from within.

A New Covenant people need to reign in a New Covenant way. Since we are 'not under law but under grace' (Romans 6:14), we cannot reign in life by legalistically obeying all sorts of external evangelical laws. There is only one way to overcome – and it has nothing whatsoever to do with actions. Those who reign in life are, amazingly, not those who strive to do better but those who:

receive God's abundant provision of grace and of the gift of righteousness (Romans 5:17).

The Old Covenant focus was on performance, and Jesus' performance completely satisfied his Father. If God looks on his Son and through him accepts us, how can we gain God's extra approval by returning to a treadmill of dead works? We can't.

The New Covenant focus is not on performance but on position. Through the cross Jesus has lifted us up into a reigning position. We are seated with him in heavenly places (Ephesians 2:6) and are accepted in the One God loves (Ephesians 1:6).

Others may try to impose 'religious laws' upon us – we may even try to impose them upon ourselves – but God knows nothing of them. They belong to another gospel, one that has to do with legalism, not with relationship. Dutiful service is something done by slaves. Jesus said:

I no longer call you servants ... Instead, I have called you friends (John 15:15).

He wants us not only to adopt the name of friends but to live like them with a new motivation: not law but love; doing things not because we ought to but because we want to.

So give up the legalistic Christian striving! It will not impress God any more than the good works you did before you trusted Jesus. Instead, rejoice in the knowledge that reigning in life flows from receiving God's abundant provision of grace and of the gift of righteousness. And live in the good of what Christ has already done for you!

2

Mrs Law and Mrs Grace

The pious Jews of Jesus' time thought that salvation was obtained through meticulous observance of the law. By 'law' they meant not only the Old Covenant commands given to Moses, but a large number of additional laws as well. These extra regulations had sprung up from their interpretation of the law. Thus they tithed not only their incomes but their mint, dill and cummin as well (Matthew 23:23).

As we read the New Testament, it becomes increasingly apparent that the Pharisees were totally bound by the demands of the law. This fact is most clearly evident in their encounters with Jesus.

- Note the Pharisees' preoccupation with the law in: Matthew 12:2; 12:10; Mark 10:2; Luke 20:22; John 5:10.

Today unbelievers think that Christians are people who are just as locked into rules as the Pharisees were. They reason that this being the case, it would be better to enjoy life now and become a Christian when they are older and need God more.

Although believers would agree that their lives are not controlled by laws as the Pharisees' were, they may wonder what response to give if they were asked the question: 'Are Christians under the law or not?' After all, didn't Jesus say that he had come to uphold the law?

• Do you think that Christians are under the law?

Mr Law

The apostle Paul responds to this question by giving us an illustration. 'Mankind,' he says, 'is the wife of a husband called law' (Romans 7:1–6). Mr Law has us totally under his thumb. He tells us where we are wrong and is constantly commanding us, 'Do this, don't do that.' An austere, condemning figure, he never lifts so much as a finger to help us fulfil his requirements. He is also always right. When he says something, there is no further argument. It's law!

The situation is made even more grim when you consider that Mrs Law cannot simply go off and marry someone else. We may see and want to live with Jesus but we know we would be committing spiritual adultery if we left our present husband (Romans 7:2, 3). We are not free agents. Mr Law has bound us to him till death us do part. He will himself never pass away (Matthew 5:18) and we cannot do away with him.

Dying to be discharged from law

There is only one answer to our problem:

you … died to the law through the body of Christ
(Romans 7:4).

Our death through Christ has broken the marriage bond to law. We are therefore free to join ourselves to another husband.

This release from the law is absolutely clear-cut and can be likened to a soldier's discharge from the army. Until a certain date the young recruit is sub-jected to all the rigours and disciplines of military training. He is under orders which he is expected to obey to the letter.

But on the day of his discharge, he strolls care-lessly across the parade ground, a free man. Horrified at the sight of this slovenly soldier, the sergeant bellows out to him the command to return and stand to attention. At first the ex-soldier cringes at the familiar cry. Then he remembers that this man, once his superior, no longer has any authority over him. He raises a hand and waves goodbye. The sergeant can yell for all he is worth, it is of no consequence. He cannot order around someone who has been discharged. The answer to the question, 'Are Christians under law?' is 'No'.

• Read I Timothy 1:9.

- For whom is the law designed?

The law is not for believers, because they are dead to it (Galatians 2:19) and have been totally discharged from their service to it. Mr Law can continue to make endless demands of us if he wishes, but if we know where we stand, he will receive no response from us.

The Colossian believers did not fully understand this complete freedom from law. Having been released, they were submitting again to rules and regulations.

- Read Colossians 2:21.

- What were these rules and regulations?

Paul had to point out that these actions had the external appearance of wisdom but were of no internal value (Colossians 2:22,23).

Instead of trying to produce a godly life in Christians by imposing rules upon them, he reminds them of their new position in Christ and tells them to live out their new life (Colossians 3:1–5).

When Paul talks to the Corinthians about sexual immorality, he does not refer to the law and say, 'You shall not commit adultery.' Instead, he tells them that their bodies are temples of the Holy Spirit (1 Corinthians 6:19) and reasons that this being the case, they should honour God with their bodies (1 Corinthians 6:20). He uses a New Covenant argument, not an Old Covenant one!

Similarly, when Paul speaks to them about a special offering for the poor, he makes no reference to the Old Testament laws.

I am not commanding you, but I want to test the sincerity of your love (2 Corinthians 8:8).

His request for financial help is not based on obedience to law but on devotion to Christ. Paul reminds the Corinthians that Jesus gave up his riches for them and that their giving is a natural response to this.

So when faced with any issue, we approach it not from a 'Thou shalt/Thou shalt not . . .' Old Testament perspective. We apply New Testament principles and work out from these how God would like us to act.

Mr Grace

We have died to Mr Law not so that we can go off to do our own independent thing, and simply be a free agent, but so that we 'might belong to another' (Romans 7:4). That person is Jesus.

The difference between the two husbands is phenomenal. Mr Law was an overbearing and demanding individual. He wearied and burdened us with rules yet refused to help us. Jesus, on the other hand, is 'gentle and humble in heart' and he gives us rest for our souls, an easy yoke and a light burden (Matthew 11:29,30).

Jesus can offer his bride something that the law

could never offer her: love. Jesus left his heavenly Father and earthly mother to be joined to us and he suffered an agonising death on the cross to win us. When the Father sees his Son's choice of bride, he approves and agrees that we were chosen for Jesus from the foundation of the world.

Our new husband is everything we could wish for. He shares his whole life with us, shows concern for our welfare, offers us sympathy, protection, mercy and grace. He showers us with spiritual and material gifts and, when we need help, he listens and intercedes with his Father on our behalf.

Truly, the bride of Christ should be ecstatically in love with her husband! He is everything she could ever wish for and he has made marvellous plans for our future in our relationship with him.

Living to be united with Christ

Not only was Mr Law incapable of loving his wife, he was also impotent and unable to give her spiritual fruit (Galatians 3:21). Laws can never produce life. They can only draw lines of right and wrong, pounce on our mistakes and put us under condemnation.

- Read Romans 7:10 and note the effect that the law had on Paul.

By complete contrast, Jesus is a life-giving, fruitful husband.

If a man remains in me and I in him, he will bear much fruit (John 15:5).

This statement reflects the Father's original desire for his children to 'be fruitful and increase in number' (Genesis 1:28). The blessing of fruitfulness which once rested on Adam and Eve now rests on Jesus and his bride, the church.

Jesus wants us to have an intimate love relationship with him. The marriage is consummated when we first receive his Word and become Christians (John 15:3). Since Jesus' words are 'Spirit and life' (John 6:63), we shall bear fruit only if we allow them to dwell in us (John 15:4). As we continue to live intimately with Jesus, taking his advice in the Word, God will answer our prayers (John 15:7) and Jesus will complete our joy by making us fruitful.

- Read John 15:8 and note how the Father is affected by our fruitfulness.

Bigamy?

A wife who is happy with her new husband is usually unlikely to return to the old one. Christians, however, often fall into a terrible trap. Although we have been freed from our old husband, we find it hard to break with our former attitudes to ourselves and our negative self-worth.

Having enjoyed the glorious liberty of our new marriage, we can still become vulnerable to the pressures of feeling unworthy and even condemned. The devil then becomes very active and tries to tell us that we are not working hard enough to please our new husband.

Tragically, we believe him. Before long, we are desperately trying to please our new husband by observing the sort of rules that our old husband required of us. By doing this we hope to shake off all the feelings of condemnation.

What has gone wrong? Simple. The wife has returned to her old husband. The loving relationship she once had with Jesus has turned into a legalistic striving to fulfil the demands of evangelical law. It's spiritual adultery and it will never work.

Jesus wants to shatter our ingrained belief that to please him we must plough through a list of Christian rules and regulations. Christians have died to their relationship with law and must never allow themselves to be lured back into it.

But now, by dying to what once bound us, we have been released from the law so that we serve in the new way of the Spirit, and not in the old way of the written code (Romans 7:6).

Now is the time to turn your back on Mr Law for ever. Remove any 'dutiful striving' baggage from his house; discharge yourself from any hold he has over your life; slam the door against him; wave a final farewell and move in with Jesus. A continual love affair awaits you. Enjoy it!

• Maybe you can think of some 'religious laws' you have always felt you must keep to please God and be a 'good Christian'.

- On a piece of paper, list some things that you now know you must leave behind or view differently.

3

Christians – Sinful or Righteous?

Are you righteous? Most Christians would probably reply negatively to that question. 'Well, er . . . I wouldn't say I'm exactly righteous,' they would say modestly. 'I try to do what God wants but there's always room for improvement.' That is about as far as they would go in conversation but in private, the secret struggle to be righteous is likely to be rather more intense.

'Righteous! You? You're kidding!' The devil pounces immediately the questioner has left. 'You might do a few good things for people, read the Bible and pray now and again. But look at what you don't do! And look at what you do wrong! Even if you know that you don't reign in life by striving to please God, you certainly can't claim to have any righteousness.'

When you think about what he says, you begin to feel guilty for having suggested that there may be any righteousness in you at all. 'There is no-one righteous, not even one' (Romans 3:10) you recall. Jesus, of course, is righteous (1 John 2:1) but people are not. They are just sinners saved by grace. They can, however, do righteous, love-motivated things. It's just a pity that you in particular don't do enough of them.

Prosecution

Satan once stood beside Joshua to accuse him.

- Read Zechariah 3:3,4 and note:

- What Joshua was wearing.

- What these symbolised.

- What God said to Satan.

- What God did for Joshua.

Immediately Joshua, the high priest, came before the Lord, Satan was there to accuse. There were many things about Joshua that his adversary could have condemned but God would not have it. He silenced Satan before he could utter even one word against Joshua.

We are priests of God (1 Peter 2:9) and Satan is our accuser who is active twenty-four hours a day (Revelation 12:10).

One of his main reasons for accusing us is to stop us from bringing our priestly offering of worship to God. He is a very experienced adversary. In fact he has, over the years, almost per-

fected his technique in this particular area and
has given many unworthy believers a prison sentence of 'righteous acts'. His eloquence virtually
assures him of a guilty verdict every time he oper-
ates.

How does he work? He begins by bringing
together truths, half truths and out-of-context Bible
verses. Then he confidently presents his evidence
against us: poor prayer times, lack of love for
people and general all-round failure to live as God
wants. He pours out evidences of our wretched-
ness and in the witness box we hang our heads in
agreement and wallow in feelings of condemnation.

God silenced Satan when he tried to accuse
Joshua. Sadly we often prefer to listen to Satan! We
allow the devil to go on talking to us about our use-
lessness and totally fail to employ a defence lawyer,
let alone listen to him! 'There is no defence,' we
think. 'I'm guilty, so I've just got to get my Christian
life together.'

Defence

But bring a more skilful advocate into the courtroom and he will defend you. In fact, at this point
in the proceedings he is sitting on the edge of his
seat ready to leap up with evidence in your favour
such as the prosecution could never contradict.
And it will release you – for ever.

He objects on the grounds that God has made
an amazing arrangement which gives the accused

a 'not guilty' verdict based on the truth that there is

*no condemnation for those who are in Christ Jesus
(Romans 8:1).*

Sinners in Adam

The Bible tells us that everything God made was very good (Genesis 1:31). Sin was therefore not a natural part of creation but an invasion from the outside. Sadly, it had a drastic effect.

* **Read Romans 5:12 and note what this was.**

There is one reality that the natural man fears more than anything else: death. The rich must bow before it. So must the poor, the young, the old, the employed, the unemployed, the strong and the weak. It is an evaded subject – something you don't talk about except in jest or where it is unavoidable.

* **Read Hebrews 2:15.**

* **How does the fear of death affect people?**

When Adam sinned, we sinned. We do not remember sinning in Adam but God put his sin to our account and his verdict on us was 'guilty'. We could not escape his judgement by doing righteous acts because even our righteousness was like 'filthy rags' (Isaiah 64:6) and could never take us out of

Adam. There was only one answer. We had to be 'born again' (John 3:3).

Righteous in Christ

The Scriptures tell us that Adam is a 'pattern of the one to come' [Christ] (Romans 5:14). In other words, the way Adam's sin affected the whole human race teaches us something about how Jesus' obedience affects all who receive him and become new creatures in Christ. Adam and Christ are heads of two different races of people and what happens to them affects us.

Under the Old Covenant, an individual bringing a sacrifice to the altar was not concerned about his own appearance. He did not fear that he might have a torn or dirty coat that would attract the eye of the priest and therefore disqualify him. His pre-occupation was, 'Is the lamb that I'm offering acceptable? Will the priest find fault with it? Is it good enough for God? Will it atone for me?'

Under the New Covenant, Christians need not feel unworthy to approach God. We are not expected to rely on our own righteousness, but on Christ's. He is our sacrificial Lamb and has no blemishes or defects (1 Peter 1:19). His perfect sacrifice has fully satisfied the Father on our behalf.

We cannot add any personal righteousness to Christ's sacrifice in order to make it more accept-able to God – something which is already perfect can never be improved. This is why the Scriptures tell us that we can:

approach the throne of grace with confidence (Hebrews 4:16).

Our confidence is not in ourselves, but in the One who gave his life for us. Salvation is a gift (Romans 6:23). Immediately we receive it, we are taken out of Adam and placed into Christ. Just as our association with Adam condemned us, so our association with Christ justifies us.

• **Read and consider Romans 5:16.**

The prosecutor glares angrily at the counsel for the defence, who looks round the courtroom and questions:

Who will bring any charge against those whom God has chosen? It is God who justifies. Who is he that condemns? (Romans 8:33, 34)

• **What does Romans 8:1 tell you?**

'Ah, yes,' says the defendant, glancing nervously at the prosecutor, 'I understand that I've been taken out of Adam and placed into Christ but I still feel guilty and far from where God wants me to be.'

The counsel for the prosecution nods in full agreement but the advocate turns full attention on the defendant and continues, 'But don't you realise that you have not only been saved but credited with Christ's righteousness as well?' And the defendant listens, amazed.

- Read Deuteronomy 6:25.

- What did God require his people to do?

- What would be the result?

The apostle Paul was once 'as for legalistic right-eousness, faultless' (Philippians 3:6) but when he became a Christian, his thinking about how to be righteous totally changed.

- How would you correct the following statement?

  And be found in him [Christ] having a
  righteousness of my own that comes from the
  law, alongside that which is through faith in Christ
  the additional righteousness that comes from
  God and is by faith. (See Philippians 3:9.)

The answer to the question, 'Are you righteous?' is Yes! The evidence is in the Bible.

- Read Romans 3:21.

- What sort of righteousness has been made known?

- Read Romans 3:22; 4:5.

- How does righteousness come to us?

Righteousness comes free with Jesus! We reign in life by receiving God's abundant provision of grace and the gift of righteousness (Romans 5:17). Adam once made us sinful but now Christ makes us righteous. We are not righteous some of the time, but always. Jesus' perfect righteousness has been given to us and he is:

the same yesterday and today and for ever (Hebrews 13:8).

God only ever sees us, as Wesley's great hymn declares, 'clothed in righteousness divine'.

* **Read Romans 4:23,24.**

* **What is Paul's main point here?**

'So I object' continues the advocate, 'on the grounds that someone who has been declared righteous by God cannot be condemned as guilty. If God has declared him righteous, there is no case for him to answer since he cannot be righteous and guilty at the same time.'

The accused sits in the witness box and marvels. Suddenly he's beginning to understand that his guilt feelings do not reflect reality. He cannot try to be righteous because he *is* righteous – and that means that he cannot make himself more or even less righteous. The answer to condemnation is not sanctification but justification. All he needs to do is hide himself in Jesus. 'I thought I couldn't win,' he says to himself. 'The truth is, I can't lose.'

The prosecutor sends a barrage of fiery objections and accusations in the direction of the witness box but none of them hits its mark. The defendant is wearing the breastplate of righteousness and it silences all condemnation. Satan slips out of the building, defeated.

Jesus, our advocate, smiles and rests his case. The accused walks away from the 'law' court gloriously free, righteous and determined never to allow himself to come under condemnation again.

- Read Hebrews 7:25 and note what Jesus lives to do.

But if anybody does sin, we have one who speaks to the Father in our defence – Jesus Christ the Righteous One (1 John 2:1).

4

Law – Sinful or Good?

On the cross, Jesus received the law's condemnation and judgement. We died with him to the law and it can therefore no longer touch us. We now serve God in an altogether different way – not through new laws but through new hearts.

Since we have now been discharged from the law, we might be forgiven for wondering where it fits into God's plan. Does it actually accomplish anything? Indeed, if the law brings us into bondage, couldn't we even suggest that law and sin are equally evil? One simply aggravates the other.

The apostle Paul anticipated this question. 'Is the law sin?' (Romans 7:7) he asked. Then he utterly dismissed the notion and launched into an explanation of the purpose of the law.

It reveals sin

God has given everyone a conscience but not everyone allows it to govern their actions. People tend, rather, to bend their conscience to approve of what they want to do. So unmarried couples live together; the average person 'adjusts' his tax returns; would-be mothers murder their unborn children; and swearing, lying and drunkenness all become common, even acceptable practices.

In a society in which 'almost anything goes', people find it hard to work out what a clear conscience actually is! 'I was obeying my conscience,' said the spy Anthony Blunt, who betrayed his nation.

Although the unconverted can train their consciences to obey some sort of moral code, they need absolutes by which to measure performance. They have no clear guidelines about what's right and wrong and simply act as far as their particular conscience allows.

God's law, on the other hand, presents mankind with a definite and objective statement of what is acceptable and what is not.

Through the law we become conscious of sin (Romans 3:20).

The Pharisees thought that sin related to outward actions alone, so they tried to justify themselves by arguing that they had never committed adultery or murder. But the law also said, 'You shall not covet' (Exodus 20:17) and Jesus pointed out that this is something which goes on in the heart (Matthew 5:28). There is as much sin in the attitude as there is in the action, but you can only discover this through the law.

It was the law that showed me my sin. I would never have known the sin in my heart – the evil desires that are hidden there – if the law had not said, 'You must not have evil desires in your heart' (Romans 7:7 LB).

Everyone who sins breaks the law (1 John 3:4).

So the law thunders out God's standards. It defines the boundary lines of right and wrong and reveals to us what sin actually is.

It provokes sin

Let us say that it is a beautiful sunny day and you have decided to visit some public gardens. You put the dog in the car and when you arrive, you discover that dogs are not allowed in the gardens. Your immediate reaction is to rebel against the rule: 'My dog is perfectly well-behaved. I don't see why he shouldn't come in with me. Besides, I'll keep him on a lead.'

You stroll along the path for five minutes before you notice a number of signs along the verge. They remind you, 'Do not walk on the grass.' Until you saw them, you had no intention of walking on the grass but immediately you became aware of the rule, you actually found yourself wanting to disobey it. Sin lay dormant until it was provoked. Then something in you reacted to the desire to sin.

But sin used this law against evil desires by reminding me that such desires are wrong and arousing all kinds of forbidden desires within me! (Romans 7:8 LB)

Many people today tell us that they believe in God, but they understand him to be someone who neither imposes moral laws on them nor makes any demands of them. Tell such a person, 'The Ten Commandments require this of you,' or 'God does not approve of what you are doing,' and you are likely to receive a negative, even hostile response. Before you spoke, he was not aware of sin. It was 'dead' to him. But by telling him what the law says you have awakened a consciousness of sin which makes him feel uneasy.

It condemns sin

An unbeliever thinks he is 'alive' (Romans 7:9). He feels well, he has confidence and congratulates himself on the (possibly very moral and religious) way he is running his life.

Then one day, he hears the message of the law and feels condemned before God. All his self-reliance and self-confidence melt away. The law, having aroused an awareness of sin in him (Romans 7:9), makes him feel guilty and unclean. He is helpless, as the law resulted in his being given the death penalty (Romans 7:10).

It shows the sinfulness of sin

Romans 7:12 tells us that the law is holy, righteous and good. Just as something white reveals how filthy everything else is around it, so the pure truth forces us to acknowledge how utterly foul sin really is.

*It was sin, devilish stuff that it is, that used what was good
to bring about my condemnation. So you can see how
cunning and deadly and damnable it is. For it uses God's
good laws for its own evil purposes (Romans 7:13 LB).*

It leads us to Christ

Like unbelievers today, the Jews of Jesus' time set
their hopes on Moses who represented the law.
They thought that God had given them his law so
they could save themselves through it.

- According to Romans 9:32, why did they fail?

- Read John 5:46.

- According to Jesus, what did Moses do?

The law was never intended to be a way of salvation. Salvation is entirely a matter of grace. God
established his covenant with Abraham and it was
based not on law but on a promise (Galatians
3:18).

So why was the law brought in? It was added
later to show people their need of a covenant
of grace. In Greek culture there was a servant
who collected the children and took them to
school. In much the same way, the law is
designed to:

*lead us to Christ that we might be justified by faith
(Galatians 3:24).*

The unbeliever who leads a moral religious life is inevitably miserable. He is trapped by laws he must keep in order to remain in God's 'good books' and he lives with the condemnation which comes when he fails to keep those laws. If he ever received the truth, he would know that he is totally sinful and bankrupt. And he would realise that a 'bit of religion' is not the answer. The law points him to only one Saviour – the Lord Jesus Christ.

5

Captive to Sin?

The interpretation of Romans 7:14–25 has foxed many Christians. It is the story of a man in a battle and the controversy centres around his identity. Is the apostle Paul describing pre-Christian experience, normal Christian life or both?

Man in turmoil

The conflict is not caused by selfish rebellion in the man's heart. He is not fighting against God's law. Rather, he respects and wants to uphold it.

- Read Romans 7:14–25 and note:

- What he says about the law (vv. 14,16).

- What he desires to do (v. 18).

- How he feels about God's law (v. 22).

There is no sign of hostility here. This man totally

accepts the law. It is something agreeable and beneficial and he embraces it with his heart, mind and will.

The conflict begins only when the man tries to live out the law. Then he realises that everything in him rebels against his desire to uphold God's commands.

Note also:

- What he says about himself (v. 14).

- What he wants to do and what he does (v. 15).

- What he knows about himself (v. 18).

The man is experiencing terrible inner conflict. On the one hand, he desperately wants to do good, but when he tries, he utterly fails. The battle is between his body and his mind and it makes him a prisoner of the law of sin (v. 23).

Debate

'Paul is describing an unbeliever,' say some Christians. 'The battle which is described refers to his trying to gain salvation by good works.' 'Not so,' say other believers. 'This passage is far too close to Christian experience to be pre-conversion. The more mature you are in your walk with the Lord, the more aware of conflict you will be.' And the third opinion has a foot in each camp and declares,

'It's a paradox. We struggle both as unbelievers and as believers.'

- Before reading the rest of this chapter, what do you think?

Examination

It is all too easy to take a Bible text and test it by experience rather than look at what it actually says. A close examination of the words that Paul chooses will give us a huge clue about what he means.

The man in question is described as a prisoner in total bondage. He cannot do what he wants to do, and he does what he hates. He feels miserable and powerless to escape from the clutches of his master, Sin.

- Read verse 24 and note the desperation in his cry.

Clearly, we are not reading about someone who is telling us that he is prone to making a few mistakes. He is not just having a bad day! The strength of the language indicates that this individual is completely enslaved and in utter despair. So we must ask ourselves: Who can make such hopeless statements about himself?

Unbelievers?

Is this battle normal experience for unbelievers? Would they actually say the things that the man in Romans 7 does? It is highly unlikely.

Take Romans 7:14 for example. Here, the man says, 'We know that the law is spiritual; but I am unspiritual, sold as a slave to sin.' Frankly, no unbeliever would ever tell you that the law is spiritual. He would simply say that laws are there to prevent you from doing certain things. Like the Pharisees, he would believe that the law is concerned with wrong actions, not wrong attitudes as well.

In addition, he would in no way view himself as unspiritual and sold as a slave to sin. On the contrary, he would probably tell you that he is feeling happy, healthy, secure, self-confident and doing very nicely, thank you. By continuing to perform good works he hopes that he will justify himself.

As you read on in Romans 7, it becomes clear that no unbeliever would express himself in the same way as the man in the passage. The constant inner struggle against sin is foreign to him. He would never consider himself to be a 'wretched man' nor say, 'Nothing good lives in me.' He may be irritated by sin or dislike its consequences, but he would never hate it. And as far as the law is concerned, he would neither delight in it nor desire to honour or abide by it. Since he is a law unto himself, what he does is, according to that law, always right.

- What does Romans 8:7 say about the sinful mind?

Believers?

If the battle does not seem to apply to unbelievers, does it reflect normal Christian experience? It would be easy to conclude that this must be the case – but the issue is not quite so straightforward.

The man who states that he is imprisoned by his sin is the same one who also wrote:

We died to sin; how can we live in it any longer? . . . anyone who has died has been freed from sin . . . do not let sin reign in your mortal body . . . You have been set free from sin and have become slaves to righteousness (Romans 6:2,7,12,18).

How is it that this captive to sin, this anguished man, is exactly the same person who also advocates such amazing liberty from sin's bondage?

How can Paul be wretched and incapable of doing good one minute, and the next be declaring freedom from condemnation and victory for every believer? How can he wish the churches 'grace and peace' when he is in such turmoil? How can he exhort the Philippians to rejoice (Philippians 4:4) when he is so miserable? How can he affirm, 'I will not be mastered by anything' (1 Corinthians 6:12) when he openly confesses that he is dominated by sin? It does not make sense.

It makes even less sense when you consider his statement, 'Follow my example, as I follow the example of Christ' (1 Corinthians 11:1). Which example are we meant to be following – helpless captivity or glorious deliverance?

Strange, isn't it, that Paul's inner conflict in Romans 7 is not evident anywhere else in the entire New Testament? The apostle John, who had a very close relationship with Jesus, says nothing of a futile struggle to be holy. His comments invariably reflect not bondage to sin but release from it.

- Try to work out what these verses *should* say before you look them up:

  Everyone who lives in him keeps on sinning (I John 3:6).

  Everyone who is born of God will continue to sin, because Satan's seed remains in him; he will always go on sinning, because he is a sinner (I John 3:9).

  For everyone born of God struggles against the world. This is the battle that is waged against the world, even our works (I John 5:4).

As far as John is concerned, the normal Christian experience does not centre around an increasing sense of sin-consciousness. He argues, rather, that since we have God's nature in us, sin is foreign to our way of life – something occasional, not usual. If we do wrong, there is no subsequent battle for deliverance to be fought. We immediately go to Jesus who will hear our confession and forgive us completely (1 John 1:9; 2:1).

- Note what Jesus said in John 8:34,36.

When we become Christians we are no longer slaves under sin but masters over it. There is no sense in which the more spiritually mature we are, the more we will experience inner turmoil. If this were the case, the main effect of the gospel would be to increase our misery – an impossible conclusion in the light of this statement made by Paul:

We ... are being transformed into his likeness with ever-increasing glory, which comes from the Lord, who is the Spirit (2 Corinthians 3:18).

Furthermore, if misery were the order of the day, we should be forced to assume that Jesus' promise of 'life to the full' (John 10:10) actually meant 'you will have a life full of vain strugglings against your sins and shortcomings'! If it were true, this would hardly be an attractive message for unbelievers and it would not do much to encourage Christians either!

Answer

What are we to make of this? Are we to assume that Paul had drunk a little too much wine before he wrote this section in his letter to the Romans?! No! Although it is not initially obvious, there is an answer.

Paul has already told us that the law both increases sin and kills us (Romans 7:5,13). These are radical statements to make about something which was thought to bring salvation, and there would probably be objections. The apostle anticipates these and decides to use drama to illustrate his point. He therefore takes a man – any man – and uses him to reveal the law's complete inability to save, justify or sanctify us.

The man in the passage is under intense conviction of sin. The Spirit has shown him the holiness of the law and he has suddenly become aware of his own weakness and inability. Rather than receive the grace of God (Christ and the Holy Spirit are not mentioned), he thinks that he must struggle to keep the law in his own strength. The battle that ensues leads him into frustration, condemnation, despair, bondage and ultimate failure.

'And that,' says Paul, 'is what the law will do for you if you try to keep it!' So do not argue from Romans 7 that Paul experienced defeat and therefore so will you. The passage is not a hiding place to justify defeat. It is there to remind you that the law is utterly bankrupt. If you try to work out your salvation by reference to the law, you will end up in complete turmoil. So stay with your new husband!

6

Dead to Sin

Think for a minute. If God always sees us clothed in Christ's perfect righteousness, then we can sin and still be righteous! We can push our way to the head of the bus queue, ignore the old lady at the kerbside, kick the cat, lie, cheat, swear and be thoroughly nasty to everyone – and yet remain righteous! The grace of God seems to give us full permission to sin! In fact, the more we sin, the more we will prove the greatness of God's grace. What an amazing thought!

'What a ghastly thought!' (Romans 6:2 PHILLIPS) declares the apostle Paul to this suggestion. To step from 'righteousness by law' into 'righteousness by sin' is the most horrendous idea! Once we have understood the amazing extent of God's grace, we do not take advantage of it; we live in the strength of it. God wants us to live holy lives, but this holiness comes not through our own endeavours but from what God has done for us in Christ.

Pursued by a slave master

Sadly, many believers very much want to be winners but find in practice that they are fighting a losing battle. They thought that when they became Christians they would leave behind their sinful ways, but they discover that this is not always the case. Day by day they are pursued by their sins, which frequently catch up, dig their claws in and refuse to be shrugged off.

The individual who is overwhelmed in this way experiences a sort of half-salvation. It is 'Christian life at the mercy of terrible lusts, envy and other wrongs'. 'I'm just a forgiven sinner,' he says to himself. And when he feels challenged about his sins, he hangs his head in shame but does not know how to get himself free. 'I know that God sees me as righteous through the blood of Jesus,' he agrees, 'but how can I ever be free from the power of sin?'

The children of Israel once lived in slavery in Egypt. On the night of their deliverance they put blood on their door-frames and were protected from death. Although saved from judgement by the Passover blood, they still found that they were not free from their Egyptian slave masters. The Red Sea prevented their progress into full liberty. What a terrible plight! What is the good of knowing that God has passed over your sins if you are still in slavery?

Wonderfully, God opened the Sea before them and they went down into the valley and out the other side – free men! The water then swept back behind them and wiped out Pharaoh's army.

- Read Exodus 14:28 and note how many Egyptians survived.

The 'forgiven sinner' mentioned earlier has been saved by Christ's blood but is in the same state as the Israelites before they crossed the Red Sea. His slave master, Sin, is constantly in hot pursuit. He must realise that there is total freedom for him as he 'goes down' into the death which the Red Sea represents. But what does this really mean for us and what must the Christian actually do?

Over the Red Sea

We 'escape' from besetting sins only when we discover the truth that just as we have died to the law, so too have we died to sin (Romans 6:2). Paul said:

Don't you know that all of us who were baptised into Christ Jesus were baptised into his death? (Romans 6:3)

People are either in Adam or they are in Christ. There is no middle position. It is not true to say that some exceptional Christians have had a 'death to sin' experience and that all other believers should seek this experience in order to be set free. The Scriptures make it clear that everyone who is in Christ has been crucified with him (Romans 6:6; Galatians 2:20). If we have been united with him in his death (Romans 6:5), we have also been freed from sin (Romans 6:7). A corpse never feels the tug of sin. It does not feel jealous or angry or envious. You can insult it, but it is 'dead to sin'.

Do you realise that God says that you have been crucified with Christ? You might protest that if God knew about your bad temper or your unclean imagination, he would not say that your old self had been crucified. It seems very much alive! But this is where faith must play its part.

We have no trouble believing that two men were crucified with Christ, because that's what the Bible says. So when the same Bible says that we have been crucified with Christ, we have no reason not to believe what it says.

We do not remember dying with Christ any more than we recall sinning in Adam. We simply believe the Bible when it says that what happened to them is accredited to us. When we understand that we were included in Jesus' death to sin we shall actually experience freedom from sin.

On the other side

The Christian life is nothing to do with 'always trying to hold down your sinful nature'.

- Read Romans 6:6,7.

- What has happened to our 'old self'?

- What has happened to our 'body of sin'?

- What should we no longer be?

- Why does sin hold no further grip on our lives?

Although other translations carefully distinguish between the 'flesh' and the 'sinful nature' or 'old man', the New International Version uniquely and unhelpfully translates 'flesh' as 'sinful nature'. As a Christian you will inevitably have to battle against fleshly desires, but you will never have to strive to overcome your sinful nature – because you do not need to hold down something that is already dead! You are not a mere 'forgiven sinner' but a wonderful 'new creation'. You are a radically transformed being and have total liberty from all bondage to sin.

The woman caught in adultery was condemned by the law until she was brought to Christ. Jesus, who is the end of the law, did not rebuke her.

- Read John 8:11.

- What did Jesus release her to do?

In a similar way, God has completely released you from sin's controlling power. Although you are still capable of sinning, you do not have to sin any more. Jesus' words to the woman are spoken to you.

To overcome in any area of our Christian life, we start by believing God's Word, then we act on what we believe. This is exactly what Abraham did when God told him that he would be a 'father of many nations' (Genesis 17:5). If Abraham had reasoned this out, he would have dismissed the notion as absurd. He was a hundred years old and his wife was barren – even one son seemed a total impossibility, let alone a whole nation.

Yet he did not waver through unbelief regarding the promise of God, but was strengthened in his faith and gave glory to God, being fully persuaded that God had power to do what he had promised (Romans 4:20,21).

Now start counting

God says that we have died to sin. The first step we take is to believe that what he says is the truth. The next step is to 'count' ourselves dead to sin on a daily basis (Romans 6:11). The word 'count' in this verse is an accounting term which refers to 'putting it in that column because it goes there'.

A powerful illustration of what it means to 'reckon yourself dead to sin' came home to me when I flew into (I think it was) Spain. When I arrived, my watch told me that it was 3.00 p.m. but the people there said that in Spain it was 4.00 p.m. Did I wander round the country saying to myself, 'They're wrong – but while I'm here I suppose I've got to force myself to believe that it's 4.00 p.m.'? Of course not! In Spain it really was 4.00 p.m. So I adjusted my watch and adjusted my thinking to the reality of the situation.

When we count ourselves dead to sin we are not exerting our willpower in order to make it true. We are believing it because it *is* true. We have stepped out of Adam and into Christ. Sin is powerless to control us. As you believe this truth and consistently reckon on its releasing power, you will experience the freedom that Jesus promised you.

This is the victory that has overcome the world, even our faith (1 John 5:4).

7

Alive to God

Not only are we urged to consider ourselves dead
to sin, we are also exhorted to count ourselves alive
to God (Romans 6:11). This has to do with the way
we use our bodies. Will we pursue unholy desires
or let God manifest his holiness through us?

Jesus was given a body by his Father (Hebrews
10:5) and was willing to live in it. He expressed his
dedication to God through his physical body –
reaching out to people in their need, sacrificing
physical comforts and finally allowing his body to
be tortured and crucified.

He bore our sins in his body on the tree (1 Peter 2:24).

Paul urges us:

*Offer your bodies as living sacrifices, holy and pleasing to
God (Romans 12:1).*

He does not command us to surrender our bodies.
Rather, he reminds us of the amazing mercy of God

towards us and effectively asks, 'In the light of this, how can we do anything else but offer our bodies to him? We have been given blessing upon blessing: freedom from sin, deliverance from law and condemnation, the gift of righteousness, complete security in Christ, love, peace, joy, purpose . . . Surely the giving of our bodies back to God is only a natural love response to all that he has done for us in Christ.'

- From the following misquoted verse, consider how God could have rescued us from our sin:

  For God felt so duty-bound to the world that he reluctantly thought he'd better give his Son, that whoever follows his laws shall not perish but have eternal life (John 3:16).

It is not God's desire that we offer our bodies to him out of a sense of cold obligation – 'The Bible says do this, so I'd better obey.' He wants us to adopt the attitude of his Son who willingly and wholeheartedly gave himself for us – not because he was compelled to do so, but because he loved us and wanted to.

- Consider Paul's comment in 1 Corinthians 6:19,20.

The holy life is not automatic. Our wills are involved. We have to choose whether we use our bodies as if they belonged to us, or to God.

Our way of life will reflect the decision we have made.

Victory over sin

Having told the Romans that they were dead to sin, Paul said:

Do not let sin reign in your mortal body so that you obey its evil desires (Romans 6:12).

Sin wants to reign in our 'mortal' bodies. Why 'mortal'? Because our bodies are the only part of us that have not yet experienced salvation. One day they will be redeemed and transformed (Romans 8:23; Philippians 3:21) but until then, we must live with them.

Before we became Christians, the devil got at the members of our bodies and caused us to sin with them.

- Consider some sins which find expression through our eyes, ears, mouth and hands.

At that time our old nature was happy to agree with our bodies to sin. But then the old sinful nature died and we were given a new righteous nature to replace it. This new nature gives us complete power over our passions. Whereas we were once totally at the mercy of our sinful desires, we now have the ability to grant or deny our bodies permission to sin. We have the power to do what unbelievers cannot. We can stop sinning with our bodies and live victoriously from the new nature.

[God] has given us his very great and precious promises, so that through them you may participate in the divine nature and escape the corruption in the world caused by evil desires (2 Peter 1:4).

Knowing that we have power over our sins, Paul can rightly exhort us:

Do not offer the parts of your body to sin, as instruments of wickedness (Romans 6:13).

- Read Ephesians 4:25–5:4 and Colossians 3:8, 9 and consider the sins which we must *not* commit.

From defeat to victory

Before sin can reign in our bodies, it has to be invited in. Before it is invited in, it comes to the door in the form of temptation.

'Knock, knock,' it says. 'I've got something here that you can't resist!' We look out of the window, see the sin we want, consider how desirable it is, open the door, receive the goods, indulge in them and later regret our action. When we give in for about the third time, we begin to allow our conscience to become dulled about it. The process of entertaining the sin continues until it moves in as a semi-permanent lodger. It is not long before that lodger is reigning as the master of the house.

- If you are in this sad position, acknowledge the besetting sin before God now.

Jesus said:

Things that cause people to sin are bound to come, but woe to that person through whom they come (Luke 17:1).

By telling us this, he made it clear that we can never avoid temptation. Even Jesus was tempted in every area (Hebrews 4:15). There is nothing sinful about being tempted. We do not, however, need to give in to it. If we think that we are powerless against our sin, we are mistaken. If we have allowed sin to come in and reign, we are sinning by choice – because we like it – and not because we cannot control ourselves.

- Correct the following statement, then look up the answer in 1 Corinthians 10:13.

  Many temptations will seize you which are uncommon to man. And God is faithful – although he may let you be tempted beyond what you can bear. But when you are tempted, he may also provide a little assistance so that you can work your way through it.

Sanctification is not achieved by our simply handing our lives over to God. It comes as we actively co-operate with him as he brings things to light that he wants us to change. Part of the secret of resisting temptation is initially to avoid putting ourselves in a position where we might be tempted. So we say to our feet, 'No, you won't go in there,' to our eyes, 'No, I'm keeping you away from this' and to our hands and ears, 'No, that's not for touching, or hearing. I will not allow you to get anywhere near it.'

And if we already feel trapped by a sin, we no longer have to settle for, 'I've done that again. I can't help it and I'll probably repeat it in the future.' Now is the time to confess God's Word against it, to declare to the sin, 'I died to you and I don't have to allow you to reign in my life any more. Find some-where else to go!'

- Read I Corinthians 9:27 and note what Paul did.

Resisting temptation can often be a battle, but the resources are there to succeed every time.

Slaves of a new master

According to the Bible, all unbelievers are slaves to sin. They can be obvious sinners (murderers, rapists, burglars, drug addicts . . .) or respectable, good living, church-going people who have never been born again. Because these individuals are slaves, they cannot simply walk free. They need releasing.

Jesus alone releases captives from their sin. He walks into the slave market, looks around and sees you standing there filthy, in chains and under sentence of death. Then he points to you and says to the slave driver, 'I'll have that one,' and he pays the top price for your life.

Our deliverance comes when we hear God's Word, understand it with our minds, feel moved in our hearts and respond with our wills. Paul said:

Thanks be to God that, though you used to be slaves to sin, you wholeheartedly obeyed the form of teaching to which you were entrusted (Romans 6:17).

We are not saved into a sort of no-man's land, going on to move through sanctification, out of sin and into righteousness. Immediately we become Christians, we transfer from one slave owner to another.

- Consider what might be wrong with the following statement, then read Romans 6:18 to discover how it should read.

  You will be set free from sin and become slaves of righteousness.

There was a time when we gave ourselves to sin – indeed, we could not help it. He was our master and it was natural for us to obey him. Now, however, we are slaves of a new master called righteousness. The way we live will show which master we are following. John said:

If we claim to have fellowship with him yet walk in the darkness, we lie and do not live by the truth (1 John 1:6).

The man who says, 'I know him,' but does not do what he commands is a liar, and the truth is not in him (1 John 2:4).

Paul said, 'Sin shall not be your master' (Romans 6:14). This is not an exhortation but a statement of fact. We have been born of God and have his nature living in us. We are new creations for whom sin, and not righteousness, is out of character. Sin, for the Christian, is not the rule but the exception, as 1 John 2:1 makes very clear. This verse does not say: *When anybody does sin, we have one who speaks to the Father in our defence . . .*

- Look up 1 John 2:1. Note the word above that is wrong and consider how the sense of the comment changes when you alter that one word.

Since we now belong to righteousness, we must give ourselves to it. After all, it is only natural for righteous people to live righteously. So we must put behind us the lies of the enemy who continually creeps up on us and whispers, 'You can't cope with that sin, it's too great.' We are free from sin's slavery. The battle against sin has already been fought and won. The devil is a defeated foe who tries his utmost to make us think that we who are 'more than conquerors' are actually on the losing side!

But we are winners! On the one hand, we can keep the members of our bodies from sin. On the other, we can use them to perform positive acts of righteousness. Paul said:

Offer yourselves to God, as those who have been brought from death to life; and offer the parts of your body to him as instruments of righteousness (Romans 6:13).

• Read Ephesians 4:25–5:4 and Colossians 3:12–17 and consider the righteous things which we are encouraged to do.

God tests us by our actions. Are we really acting like living sacrifices who are presenting our bodies to God in worship? Are we really loving our enemies; filling in forms accurately; speaking wisely; giving the required number of hours to our jobs and treating our families well? Or are we, like the Jews in the time of Malachi, giving God any old thing?

• Read Malachi 1:6–14.

• What were the people bringing to God's altar?

• Was God pleased with them?

• What sort of offerings did he expect to receive?

The Father is no longer looking for dead animals but living sacrifices; not sloppy lives but instruments of glory and praise in the earth. He was pleased with Jesus' perfect sacrifice of himself and longs for us to imitate him. By living righteously, we are not striving to become righteous but demonstrating that righteousness is already within us. By producing fruit that not only looks righteous but tastes of righteousness, we will prove that we are slaves of righteousness and be truly useful to God.

The new slave master will tell us when we go wrong. If we do not obey him, we will experience his firm but loving hand of discipline.

- Read Hebrews 12:5.

- What should we not do?

- What does God do?

The more we continue to live for God, the more we will discover the inherent righteousness working within us. Then we shall find ourselves increasingly switching off to sin and moving forward in righteousness and victory. This is what Paul meant when he said:

Walk by the Spirit, and you will not carry out the desire of the flesh (Galatians 5:16 NASB).

Sin will make you feel wretched and inconsistent with the righteousness which God is developing in you. You have been delivered from sin to serve righteousness. Tune into your new master and be:

filled with the fruit of righteousness that comes through Jesus Christ – to the glory and praise of God (Philippians 1:11).

8

Legalism, Licence and Discipline

Matthew and Simon may both be Christians in the same church, but they have very different expectations in their day-to-day relationship with God.

Matthew has been taught that daily duties are extremely important if he wants to grow as a Christian. He therefore sets his alarm for 6.00 a.m. and gets up soon after it rings. He may be feeling like a piece of chewed string, but he refuses to let that deter him and rob him of the hour he has got to spend with God. 'Jesus expects me to follow his example,' he says to himself and then quotes Mark 1:35.

- Look this up and note the example that he's trying to follow.

Matthew reads through the Bible passage for the day, prays for the people on his prayer list and goes off to work. He hopes that he is impressing God as he replaces his desires for physical comfort

– a cosy bed and extra sleep – with spiritual activities. The church leaders all know that he is serious about his relationship with God and Matthew feels sure that God will bless him for his devotion.

Simon hates spiritual discipline! He rarely sets his alarm, but if he does, the chances are that when it wakes him up, he will switch it off, turn over and go straight back to sleep! If he has had a particularly late night, he will not think twice about staying in bed until the last possible minute. 'I'm under grace, so I don't need to go through all those stuffy spiritual rituals,' he says to himself and then quotes Galatians 5:1.

- Look this up and note why he thinks this way.

Simon happily involves himself in church activities and evangelism but has no time for anything which has the merest whiff of legalism attached to it. He does read the Bible and pray – but not on a regular basis. Spiritual endeavours like this can be done anywhere. They have to be fitted round his many other pursuits and frequently get left out altogether. The church leaders see Simon as an easy-going Christian and he rejoices that he is free in Christ not to engage in rigid daily routines.

- Which of these two people do you relate to most?

Matthew versus Simon

The trouble is that neither Matthew nor Simon has got it right. Matthew thinks that he is disciplined when he is, in fact, bound by legalism. He has a superb relationship with his Bible and prayer list but would be taken off guard if you ever said to him, 'Tell me about your relationship with Jesus.'

The request is a problem because although Matthew regularly has a devotional hour, he rarely considers the quality of it. For him, the overriding concern lies not so much in 'enjoying Jesus' presence' as in 'having a regular time'. The two are vastly different.

If he were honest with you, Matthew would tell you that his devotional times are actually thoroughly boring. He sees them as tasks that Christians should do and that good feelings are of secondary importance. 'You have to get on with them,' he affirms. 'And you believe that God will reward you because he sees your secret devotion.'

Simon, on the other hand, thinks that he is free from legalism when he is, in fact, at the mercy of indiscipline. He covers his tracks by being involved in all sorts of Christian activities, but lacks depth of character and tends to be very shallow in his understanding of God. He would feel very uneasy if you asked him, 'What has Jesus been saying to you recently?'

The question is a problem because Simon never really spends long enough with Jesus to find out what he is saying. He rarely stops to question if he is actually doing what God wants. Rather, he assumes that if an activity seems right, then it is probably OK to engage in it.

If he were honest with you, Simon would tell you that behind the scenes, his Christian life is really something of an aimless mess. He does Christian things but has never disciplined himself to spend time working out the purpose and direction of his life. He 'muddles through' but plans no definite goals. 'You must be yourself,' he says. 'The early church did not have Bibles. They just lived from what they felt.' Sadly he fails to realise that the early church was devoted to the apostles' teaching, told to treat doctrine very seriously and encouraged to guard the gospel which they had received.

Be disciplined

Christians who have the most satisfying experience of God have refused to allow themselves to be either controlled by laws or guided by feelings. They have learnt discipline.

When Paul wrote to Timothy he stressed the value of discipline by referring to a soldier, an athlete and a farmer (2 Timothy 2:4–6).

- Consider the sort of disciplines that each of these individuals needs to embrace.

It is clear that soldiers, athletes and farmers can never be effective in their professions if they do not discipline themselves. In the same way, Christians cannot serve God to their full potential unless they take seriously the need for discipline. Indeed, if you look back at outstanding men and women of God, they all practised and insisted on the need for personal discipline.

Discipline is nothing to do with trying to impress God by outward Christian conduct. It is, instead, a natural response from our hearts to his love for us. We discipline ourselves not because we have got to, but because we want to. No one forces us to set the alarm clock. We do it voluntarily – because we look forward to spending time with Jesus.

Without discipline we can crowd out times with the Lord Jesus and with our families. I find that I have a very disciplined attitude to Monday, my day off, which I set aside to be with Wendy, my wife. Although I love being with Wendy, it would frequently be possible, if I were not disciplined, to make appointments on Mondays – so I make sure I do not. This is not the law telling me 'Thou shalt not . . .' lose time with your wife, but the grace of God from within teaching me to say 'No' (Titus 2:11,12) to other distractions. It is a carefully kept discipline motivated by love and joy.

Paul once thought that he could gain credit with God by striving to be righteous (Philippians 3:5,6). When he realised that Christ's righteousness was a gift, he gave up trying to attain it by human effort, but he did not stop working hard, as is clear from 1 Corinthians 15:10:

But by the grace of God I am what I am, and his grace to me was not without effect. No, I worked harder than all of them – yet not I but the grace of God that was with me.

Why did Paul continue to work hard? Because he was now motivated not by law but by grace – and grace shows itself in hard work. Motivation is the key. Legalism speaks to us from outside and declares, 'You've got to do this.' Licence is influenced by society and protests, 'You haven't got to do anything.' But discipline springs from within and says, 'I want to do it.'

Jesus said, 'This is eternal life: that they may know you, the only true God, and Jesus Christ whom you have sent' (John 17:3). Jesus is not after your body, he is after your heart – because he knows that when he has your heart, you will willingly give him your body as well. He loves you and wants you to enjoy his company – not endure it! So discipline yourself to spend time with him and resist every attempt of the enemy to drag you into legalism or licence.

- What disciplines would you like to pursue? Write them down on a piece of paper under the following headings:

- Spiritual (e.g. Bible study, giving).

- Mental (e.g. reading, extra training).

- Physical (e.g. exercise, diet).

- Other (e.g. debt settling, hospitality, attendance at meetings).

- Pray about these things, then write down how you think you will establish them.

9

Worldliness

Charles Wesley, as we said earlier, longed for the world to taste and see the riches of God's grace. What the world more often tastes and sees is something very different. Society is led to believe that Christianity is just a matter of 'being good'. And if you are very religious, you will go to church regularly and observe a lot more legalistic rules than the normal so-called believer.

When you really begin to grasp something of the wonder of God's grace, you realise how far away the world has drifted in its understanding of Christianity. But why has this happened? Simple. Rather than offer a completely revolutionary code of life to the world, Christians have almost unconsciously allowed the world to dictate its code of life to them. When the church adopts worldly practices, society is bound to come to the wrong conclusion about the nature of God's grace, and about the true definition of worldliness. Clearly, believers need to embrace a lifestyle and a way of thinking which accurately reflect the grace of God working in them. They must never give in to worldliness.

- Read 2 Peter 3:17,18.

- If we are not careful, what can happen to us?

- How do we protect ourselves?

What's worldliness?

What people have done to avoid worldliness! The fourth-century hermits withdrew from society and wandered around the desert pursuing lives of self-denial. They prayed, meditated, fasted, went without sleep and sometimes even walled themselves up in caves. The illiterate Simeon Stylites actually spent the last part of his life on top of a pillar in Syria, and Daniel, who followed him, spent thirty-three years on a column near Constantinople.

Even today in some Christian circles there is the feeling that to avoid worldliness, you need to withdraw from society. So we see the establishment of Christian communities in ranches and farms in the countryside. The people in them pursue a self-sufficient and somewhat austere lifestyle – working on the land, eating its produce and emphasising spiritual disciplines.

Some people feel that they need to live apart from the world because the Bible teaches that association with it is something evil. They use the fol-

lowing verses to back up their opinions: 1 John 5:19,
1 John 2:15, James 4:4.

- Look up these verses to see what they're getting
  at.

So should we seriously consider taking ourselves
away from the evil influences of the world in order
to enjoy a more fulfilling spiritual experience?
Surely the answer to that proposition hinges on
another question, namely, 'What is worldliness?'
You cannot avoid something unless you know
what it really is.

The world

David recognised that:

*The earth is the Lord's, and everything in it, the world, and
all who live in it (Psalm 24:1).*

Even though the world has been cursed, it still
remains a beautiful place. The psalmist often med-
itates on the wonderful things around him and
praises God for his creative power (Psalm 104).

When John says to Christians, 'Do not love the
world,' he is not saying, 'Do not appreciate your
physical surroundings any more.' The word
'world' here is better translated 'age'. John is telling
us not to get wrapped up in something which is
really only a passing phase to which neither we nor
Jesus belong.

They are not of the world any more than I am of the world (John 17:14).

We are born from above. Our home is in heaven, but for the time being, we have to live in the world. Indeed, Jesus never expected us to be removed from it. He prayed only that we would be protected from the evil one while we remained here (John 17:15).

So what is worldliness? Is it about smoking, getting drunk at parties, swearing, cheating and the like? These may be the more obvious manifestations of worldliness, but they do not hit at the root of the problem.

In Noah's time, God judged the world by water. When Lot was alive, the judgement was by fire. We know that on both occasions the people deserved their punishment. It does, however, seem strange that the brief New Testament account of the two judgements makes no reference to what we would call 'really wicked things'. If we were telling the story, we would probably justify God's action by illustrating the extent of the people's sinfulness. But this is not the case.

- Read Luke 17:26–29 and consider the crimes of the people.

Why didn't Luke comment on the people's wickedness? Because their sin was not rooted in action but in attitude.

A worldly Christian does not necessarily do blatantly evil things. He simply carries on without any particular reference to God. He fills his mind with this age and lives as though today were everything.

Don't let the world around you squeeze you into its own mould (Romans 12:2 PHILLIPS).

The apostle Paul realised that the New Testament Christians were living in great danger of allowing the world to control them. His concern extends to believers today. We are living under tremendous pressure to conform to the standards of society. God is calling us not to remove ourselves physically from worldly influences, but to resist the temptation to exclude him from our daily lives.

So what does the Bible itself point to as the true roots of worldliness?

Worldly wealth

'What's it worth?' 'Money talks.' 'The cheque's in the post.' 'It's a cash purchase.' 'Cross my palm with silver.' 'Cash in hand.' 'Make it worth my while.' Have you ever realised just how many expressions there are about money? And have you noticed that a large number of them appeal to self-centredness: 'I'll do this for you if you give me . . .', 'I want that, so if you get it for me you'll do yourself a favour'?

• Consider Judas' question in Matthew 26:15.

It is hardly surprising that we have so many phrases. Money is, and always has been, society's most important commodity. People enter competitions to win it, they steal, cheat and strike to have it, dream about it, bribe with it and live for it. Sometimes they are even prepared to betray their friends for the sake of a handful of coins.

- What, according to Ecclesiastes 10:19, is society's view of money?

It is to this money-conscious, money-craving world that Jesus declares:

You cannot serve both God and Money (Matthew 6:24).

Money has the power to corrupt. Some people have fallen in love with it and have:

wandered from the faith and pierced themselves with many griefs (1 Timothy 6:10).

If we want to live wholeheartedly for God, we will inevitably find ourselves swimming against a very strong current of opinion. People will expect us to live for what we can get out of the world, not for what we can put into it. 'Move away and take that promotion,' they will say. 'You deserve the extra money.'

There is nothing wrong with promotion, but if you accept it only because it will give you more money, you are basing your decision on money principles. But what about your Christian testimony? Is there a good church near that new job?

And, more importantly, does God actually want you to take the promotion at all?

'But,' you will say, 'if I don't accept the promotion, the people I work with will think I'm crazy.' Exactly! But you are not conforming to their world of money because you live in another kingdom. It is more important for you to do what God wants than what people expect.

Worldly wisdom

Paul warned the Corinthians:

If any one of you thinks he is wise by the standards of this age, he should become a 'fool' so that he may become wise (1 Corinthians 3:18).

Eve believed that the fruit of the forbidden tree was 'desirable for gaining wisdom' (Genesis 3:6), so she ate it and suffered the consequences.

'You don't really believe all that nonsense about Adam and Eve, do you?' say intelligent people. 'How naïve can you get? These days you should be more scientific about things. You're just so gullible you'll believe anything!'

Interesting, isn't it? The very people who condemn you for your 'foolishness' at the same time condemn themselves for their 'wisdom'! Although denying any belief in Genesis 3, they commit exactly the same sin as Eve did. They believe that they can gain wisdom apart from God and reach out for it where it cannot be found! Unless they join God in his 'foolishness', they will never be wise!

- Consider what Paul says in I Corinthians 1:18.

Worldly wisdom would state that it is ridiculous to pin your hopes on the life and death of someone who was crucified in the Middle East nearly two thousand years ago.

Modern thinking argues the irrelevance of trusting your destiny to the stories of fishermen and tax collectors regarding the life of a 'faith healer' called Jesus of Nazareth.

Modern thinkers have even shaken Christendom with their fine sounding arguments. 'It's impossible to believe in an actual physical resurrection from the dead,' they confidently declare. 'Somehow the resurrection of Jesus should be interpreted in other ways.'

- What is Paul's reply to them in I Corinthians 15:14?

They assert that the church will never attract modern thinkers in the world unless we abandon old ways of presenting Christ. 'We must not offend the intellects of modern man,' they say.

- Try to correct the following statement from memory, then check your answer in I Corinthians 1:21.

  For since in the wisdom of man the world through its wisdom came to know God, God was pleased through the logic of what was preached

to save those who worked things out
intellectually.

Mankind hates the simple message of the cross. It
insults the intelligence to receive salvation by faith
alone, so modern theologians make the way to God
more 'acceptable'. 'Jesus was an excellent ethical
teacher,' they say. 'We do well to follow his
example.'

This sort of thinking is characteristic of the spirit
of this age. Human pride states, 'You have to
understand God scientifically. We're not actually
meant to do exactly what the Bible says. That's not
sensible.' Humanly speaking it may not be sensible
to follow what God says in his Word, but that's the
secret of it. God's foolishness is greater than man's
wisdom – and we are called to be committed not to
man's ways but to God's.

Human pride argues that Paul was only a man of
his age and was therefore limited in his understanding. We must suspect his writings in the light
of our modern insights.

We will find out whether our attitudes are
'worldly' or biblical by seeing how we personally
respond to clear biblical teaching which differs
from modern thinking. For instance, Paul taught
that a wife should submit herself to her husband
as to the Lord, for the husband is head of the
wife as Christ is head of the church (Ephesians
5:22–24).

• Do you think she should submit or not?

Worldly wisdom will say to us, 'You can't afford to give away any money this month.' But what does God say?

- Correct the following statement, then check your answer in Luke 6:38.

  Hold back, and it will be given to you. An adequate measure will come in your direction. For with the measure you would have used, it will be measured to you.

Worldly wisdom will say to us, 'That man has been perfectly horrible to you. Now's your chance to get even with him.' But what does God say?

- Correct the following statement, then check your answer in Luke 6:27,28.

  Hate your enemies, harm those who hate you, curse those who curse you, resent those who ill-treat you.

Worldly wisdom will say to us, 'Aim to be a big name. Be seen in all the right places. Do all things that will make people see how good you are. It doesn't matter how many toes you tread on to get there – just push hard.' But what does God say?

- Correct the following statement, then check your answer in Matthew 18:4.

Whoever gets himself noticed like a king is the
greatest in the kingdom of heaven.

Whenever you face an issue, you choose whether
you apply to it man's wisdom or God's foolishness.
It's a step of faith to push aside the obviously sensible words of men and to put total confidence in
the apparently illogical Word of God. Paul told the
Corinthians:

*We have conducted ourselves ... not according to worldly
wisdom but according to God's grace (2 Corinthians 1:12).*

Worldly religion

Religious people say that to get away from worldliness, you have to follow certain Christian rules. In
this way you will prove that you are not worldly. In
other words, you must go to church on Sunday, you
mustn't go to parties, you mustn't drink or smoke,
wear outrageous clothing or play football on Good
Friday.

All these things may appear to be commend-
able, but they are of no value to us whatsoever
in escaping worldliness (Colossians 2:20–23).
Man-made laws are forced on us from outside.
They are worldly ways of trying to be spiritual.
Follow them and you may salve your conscience
but you will remain worldly because you are not
motivated by the Spirit of God working within
you.

• Read Galatians 4:9–11.

- What was Paul's fear?

- What were the Galatians doing to make him so concerned?

So, according to the Bible, how do we escape world-liness? We shall see in the next chapter.

10

Escape from Worldliness

How do we escape worldliness? Should we, like John the Baptist, live frugally away from the world? No. Before John was even born, he was given his ministry by God (Luke 1:14–17). His life fulfilled specific prophecy and there is no way that we can turn his experience into the 'normal Christian life'.

Indeed, it is probable that John expected the Messiah to imitate him by eating spartan meals, abstaining from wine and living well away from people. So when he heard that Jesus was actually eating with, drinking with and living among sinners, John naturally began to doubt if Jesus really was the Messiah. And he sent his disciples to find out (Matthew 11:2,3).

But Jesus cannot be removed from his people. 'His name is Immanuel – which means God with us' (Matthew 1:23). Jesus was the most unworldly person who ever lived on earth, yet he did not withdraw from society and become a hermit. He could not do that – because he was sent not to poles but

to people; not to caves but to captives; not to the
deserts but to the despairing.

We are the 'light of the world' (Matthew 5:14–16).
Jesus does not say to us, 'Let your light shine before
desert rocks, palm trees and cacti' – mainly because
these things find it difficult to respond to the
gospel! Jesus said:

*Let your light shine before men, that they may see your good
deeds and praise your Father in heaven (Matthew 5:16).*

Escapism is not the answer. We will find deliverance from worldliness . . .

Through the cross of Jesus

The world can give us nothing, so it is futile to revel
in it or put any hope in it. All the world can offer is
short-term success and precarious fulfilment.
Paul's boast is not in outward worldly things. He
glories in the cross.

For Paul, the cross was not simply a memory, nor
a sentimental symbol. For him, the cross spelt death
to all earthly hopes and aspirations. The world crucified the Lord Jesus and we are invited to take up
our cross and follow him. By taking up our cross,
we are saying that we lay down our lives in this
world for Jesus. He said:

*The man who loves his live will lose it, while the man who
hates his life in this world will keep it for eternal life
(John 12:25).*

- Read Galatians 6:14.

- How does the cross deliver us from the world's system?

Through the renewing of our minds

The Bible tells us that God doesn't see things as we do:

The Lord does not look at the things man looks at. Man looks at the outward appearance, but the Lord looks at the heart (1 Samuel 16:7).

The world is under the control of a liar. Satan wants us to wrap ourselves up in worldly thinking, to go around totally preoccupied with physical pleasures: new car, new clothes, new toys, more promotion, more money, more exotic holidays.

The kingdom of God is in the hands of someone who claimed to be 'the truth' (John 14:6). Jesus wants us to turn away from worldly thinking, to be sanctified inwardly by the truth (John 17:17). Our primary concern needs to be not, 'What will people think about this?' but 'What does God say in his Word about it?' We must learn how to reject all worldly thought patterns in favour of a completely revolutionary code of conduct.

- According to Matthew 5:3–10, what sort of people receive God's blessing?

Through doing things as if doing them for God

'Is it right to wear jeans to the Sunday meeting?'
'Should I play football on Good Friday?' 'What
about that rather violent television programme?'
These are the sorts of questions that Christians ask.
But God does not want to take our long list of
enquiries, tick the ones he is happy about and then
return it to us. He no longer wants us to relate to
him through external laws because his way is
through relationship. So what are the answers to
our genuine difficulties? Paul said:

Everything God created is good, and nothing is to be
rejected if it is received with thanksgiving (I Timothy 4:4).

If you want to know if a thing is good, ask yourself,
'Can I thank God for this? For example, would God
be happy to see me watching this film? Does the
peace of Christ rule in my heart (Colossians 3:15)?'
If the answer is, 'Yes,' then watch it. You may find
that half-way through, you decide that you can no
longer continue to watch and be thankful and
peaceful. Then it is time to change channels.

• **Read Ecclesiastes 3:1–8.**

If the question were asked, 'Is it right to dance?', the
answer would have to be, 'It depends on the time!'
Sometimes it is right, sometimes it is not. How infu-
riating for the Pharisee!

There are some questions which have definite

negative answers: 'Should I commit adultery?' 'Should I fiddle my taxes?' Sometimes, however, there is no hard and fast rule. 'Should I go swimming on Sunday afternoon?' If you are trying to dodge another responsibility, 'No'. But if you have the right motivation, 'Yes'. We live not for ourselves but for God and he will let us know by his Spirit what he wants us to do.

Through remembering it's a passing age

Paul tells us that 'this world in its present form is passing away' (1 Corinthians 7:31) and that the 'night is nearly over; the day is almost here' (Romans 13:12). The night began when Adam sinned and all mankind fell with him. But now day is breaking into the darkness. Why give your energies to a world that will soon be over? Why live as though planet earth were going to last for ever?

We are sons of light who belong to a heavenly kingdom which will last for ever. It is therefore out of character for us to live as sons of darkness who belong to an earthly world which will pass away. We were saved from darkness to live in marvellous light (1 Peter 2:9). That is why Paul exhorts us to:

put aside the deeds of darkness and put on the armour of light (Romans 13:12).

- What deeds of darkness does he mention? (v. 13)

- What should we do instead? (v. 14)

- How do we do this in practice? (Colossians 3:12–17)

Go! And shine with heavenly light before men in worldly darkness!

11

Be Transformed

Not only does God's grace teach us to avoid worldliness, it also encourages us to:

live self-controlled, upright and godly lives in this present age (Titus 2:12).

Escaping worldliness is pointless unless we replace it with something positive. And that has to do with thinking the right way and living according to God's will.

When Moses came down Mount Sinai, his face shone with reflected light (Exodus 34:29) but on the Mount of Transfiguration, Jesus radiated a light of his own (Matthew 17:2). When the verb translated 'transform' is used in the Epistles, it is always the same word that is used for Jesus' transfiguration on the mountain. The Bible tells us:

Be transformed by the renewing of your mind (Romans 12:2).

It does not say, 'Transform yourselves' or 'Be transformed by obedience to certain codes of conduct.'

The transformation which God wants us to experience comes from within us as we allow him to change our patterns of thinking.

Battle for the mind

If you tell someone, 'You've just won a huge sum of money in a competition,' he will be ecstatic! In the days before he receives the prize, he will be telling everyone and working out exactly what he wants to do with it. 'I'll take a holiday in the Bahamas,' he says to himself, 'and I'll move to a bigger home and buy a better car . . .'

Now imagine that the day before the man is handed his longed-for cheque, he learns that there has been a mistake and he has not won after all. Devastated, he phones up to find out what has happened. He is angry that the error was not noticed earlier and resentful towards the man who did get the prize. He sulks in self-pity and retreats to the local pub where he drowns his sorrows in several pints of beer.

Influence a person's thinking and you will always affect his reactions. That is why there is such a fierce battle for the mind. On the one hand Satan wants us to adopt negative thought patterns and live by them. On the other hand, God encourages us to:

take captive every thought to make it obedient to Christ (2 Corinthians 10:5).

The unconverted mind

Before we became Christians, our minds were under the control of the devil.

* Note from the following verses how our minds were affected.

  2 Corinthians 3:14; 4:4; Colossians 1:21.

Brilliant men and women think that they can understand God through their superior intellect and wisdom. They are mistaken. Their minds, like those of any other unbeliever, are blind. Like the Pharisees, they think that they know God but they are, in reality, groping around in darkness.

When Jesus healed the man who had been born blind, the Pharisees did not want to acknowledge the miracle. Instead, they reacted with scorn, 'hurled insults at him and said, "You are this fellow's disciple! We are disciples of Moses!"' (John 9:28) This reaction is typical of unbelievers. Their hearts are hard. They do not want to be convicted of their own blindness, but neither do they want to acknowledge that others can see (John 9:41).

Unbelievers are also hostile to the gospel. The Pharisees said to the man born blind, 'You were steeped in sin at birth; how dare you lecture us!' (John 9:34). Then they threw him out of the temple.

Before he was converted, the apostle Paul was blind, hard and hostile. Indeed, as if to emphasise the blindness of Paul's mind, God took away the apostle's physical sight. By the time Paul had emerged from his experience, he knew only too well what it was like to walk in darkness.

The converted mind

It took more than a new religion to translate Paul from a kingdom of darkness to a kingdom of light. He was forced to admit that he needed a devastating change of mind and heart, a great salvation which he could by no means work to attain.

A bit of churchgoing on Sunday and a few good deeds during the week may satisfy the human ego. They do nothing for God. Salvation does not rest on human rationalisation but on God's revelation.

When Peter told Jesus, 'You are the Christ, the Son of the living God,' Jesus replied:

Blessed are you ... for this was not revealed to you by man, but by my Father in heaven (Matthew 16:17).

- Read Matthew 11:25,26. From whom has God hidden great spiritual truths?

- To whom has he chosen to reveal them?

The transformed mind

Christians are people whose minds have been opened to the truth that they can receive salvation only as a gift from God. But this is only the beginning. Once we have been given spiritual sight, God wants us to see more and more spiritual reality. That is why Paul prays that God will give the Ephesians 'the Spirit of wisdom and revelation' and enlighten the 'eyes of [their] hearts' (Ephesians 1:17,18).

A seeing mind

In each of our lives there are areas of blindness which God wants to change. We are often not conscious of where these areas are, but they invariably stem from wrong patterns of thinking. To know the truth, we need to receive revelation from God. So when we are reading the Word or listening to a sermon, we need to be alert and praying for God to speak to us.

- Read Proverbs 2:1–5. How would God like you to react to his Word?

A willing mind

Sadly, although some people allow God to break through their hardness and bring them into the kingdom, they refuse to allow him to speak to them about certain issues. The Pharisees were unwilling to answer Jesus when he asked them if John's baptism was from God or men (Luke 20:4–8). They did not want to face the consequences of their reply to him, so they did not commit themselves to any definite opinion.

For some Christians there is a particular doctrine which they do not like. It may be water baptism, the baptism in the Spirit or some other teaching. Other believers may have been challenged about indiscipline in some area of their life or about a particular sin which they are committing. Whatever the issue, these individuals always manage to dodge it. They are unwilling to allow God to change their thinking about it because they fear the outcome.

- Read John 7:17.

If a Christian really wants God's will, he will listen to what God says. If, however, his mind is not responsive to a particular issue, he will, like the crowds around Stephen (Acts 7:57), cover his ears to block God's words. Since he has refused to receive the teaching, Jesus has no more to say to him.

James tells us that the wisdom from above is open to reason and willing to yield (James 3:17). When believers have set ways and closed minds, they demonstrate immaturity. They have prejudged a matter and have locked themselves so much into their own thinking that they absolutely refuse to listen to any other view on it. Reject hardness like this. Be willing to listen to the opinions of others and humble enough occasionally to change your mind in the light of them.

- What issue do you most try to avoid?

- Take it to God. Pray for his revelation and be open to others in your search for the truth.

A humble mind

As we grow in our knowledge of God, there is a real danger of our becoming proud of our achievements and spiritual experiences. That is why we are warned:

Do not think of yourself more highly than you ought (Romans 12:3).

However great the temptation to live for the praise of men, we must not yield to it. Paul instructs us, 'In humility consider others better than yourselves' (Philippians 2:3) and Jesus who is 'gentle and humble in heart' says to us, 'Learn from me' (Matthew 11:29).

When King David was fleeing Jerusalem a man called Shimei cursed him and pelted him with stones and dirt. David could have ordered his execution but did not. Instead, he said to his troops, 'Leave him alone; let him curse' (2 Samuel 16:11). When we are wrongly judged, God wants us to react not from wounded pride but from genuine humility. Like David, we should not seek our own revenge but entrust ourselves to God.

- Read 2 Samuel 16:12.

- Consider what David said.

- Read 2 Samuel 19:18–23.

- What did Shimei do?

One of the ways of finding out the extent of a Christian's humility is to note his response to criticism. Does he lash back and argue his point? Does he go away and sulk in self-pity? Or does he accept the negative comments and seek to learn from his ways?

• What is your usual reaction to criticism?

A thankful mind

There is always something to moan about! In fact, we get so used to complaining that we almost lose the ability to notice when we are doing it! It is second nature to us. But it is not God's nature in us. Paul said:

Do everything without complaining or arguing (Philippians 2:14).

It is all too easy to allow negative circumstances to preoccupy our thinking and make us negative people. When this happens, we lose our joy and are prone to depression and despair. We then become bitter about the situation and fail to see God's hand working in it.

• Note the wrong word in the following statement:

   We know that in most things God works for the good of those who love him (Romans 8:28).

If we really believe this (corrected) verse, we will live by it. We will not allow the devil to feed his lies into our minds and persuade us that God has with-drawn and is no longer interested. We will disci-pline ourselves to refuse to let anything shake our faith in God. He wants us to live for what we know to be true. Peter said:

Rejoice that you participate in the sufferings of Christ, so that you may be overjoyed when his glory is revealed (1 Peter 4:13).

- If you are facing a difficult situation at the moment, remind yourself that God loves you and will work out everything for your good.

A peaceful mind

We live in an anxious world. On our television screens we seem to see an increasing number of horrendous natural and man-made disasters. Earthquakes, floods, famines and wars wipe out whole cities and leave behind them complete dev-astation. Closer to home, we have our own personal problems to work out: family, friends, relation-ships, jobs, sickness – all of these threaten to over-whelm us and create within us a strong tendency to panic.

It is little wonder that so many people live on tranquillisers and sleeping tablets. Indeed, for many of them, so great is their need for such support that the world would fall apart if they acci-dentally knocked their box of pills off the bathroom shelf and into the toilet.

Jesus went through extreme pressure when he

was on earth, yet he reacted to it with a remarkable
calmness. He needed no sedatives to keep him
composed – indeed, immediately before his cruci-
fixion, he actually refused the drugged wine which
would have lessened his pain (Matthew 27:34).
How could he remain so unruffled at a time of such
distress?

- Find out from Isaiah 26:3.

Christians need never experience frenzy in the face
of pressure. Jesus exhorts us, 'Do not worry about
your life . . . Who of you by worrying can add a
single hour to his life?' (Matthew 6:25,27). And Paul
underlines these words saying, 'Do not be anxious
about anything' (Philippians 4:6).

You are capable of worrying, but can choose not
to do so. Perfect peace is freely available to you. You
will experience it as you train your mind to think
God's thoughts after him and trust him in every situation. Paul said:

The mind controlled by the Spirit is life and peace
(Romans 8:6).

Outcome

The ultimate goal of every Christian is to
become more and more like Jesus (Romans
8:29). It is an attainable goal. Jesus did not have
to live at the mercy of wrong thinking or be constantly overwhelmed by the pressures of life –

and neither do you. You can triumph by the grace of God. Let him transform your mind – and you will prove his victory in every area of your life.

12

The Will of God

Through many dangers, toils and snares
I have already come:
'Tis grace that brought me safe thus far,
And grace will lead me home.

It is God's intention that we not only receive his grace but allow it to direct the course of our lives as well. 'Continue in the grace of God,' we are exhorted (Acts 13:43). It is an ongoing process – a walk with God in the will of God – from the hour we first believed until the time he calls us home.

We have wills

Christians are not sheep without a shepherd – but some of them have a tendency to wander away from the protection that the Shepherd offers. They are the laid back believers who appear outwardly committed but are not particularly enthusiastic about giving their lives wholly to God. Instead, they simply drift about the field, nibble at Christian teaching here and there and spend more time with the flock than the Shepherd.

If you live out of earshot of the Shepherd on a daily basis, you will find it hard to hear him when you suddenly want to know his will over a major issue. Panic-stricken, you will exclaim, 'What does God want me to do?' And a confident decision which could have been born out of much practice at hearing God is, instead, the product of a lot of sleepless nights. Paul said:

Then you will be able to test and approve what God's will is (Romans 12:2).

The word 'then' is significant because it refers back to what the apostle has already said, namely, 'Offer your bodies as living sacrifices' and 'Be transformed by the renewing of your mind.' So Paul is telling us that if we first come into the fullness and blessing of God by giving him our bodies and minds, he will reveal to us his will.

God has a will

Many people in society think that God, if there is a God, wound up the world and then left it to its own devices. They and, indeed, some Christians, exist from one day to the next void of the conviction that God is controlling, organising and motivating. For them, everything that happens is almost accidental.

But when you look into the pages of the Bible

there is nowhere the impression that the world is like a big clockwork ball. On the contrary, the Scriptures are brimming with God's plans for us. One minute he is telling us, 'I'm going to do this' and the next, he does it. And God knows that all his relatively quiet day-to-day plans will reach an almighty crescendo when he brings

all things in heaven and on earth together under one head, even Christ (Ephesians 1:10).

- How would you correct the following statement?

   [God] works out some things in conformity with the purpose of his will (Ephesians 1:11).

God has a will and he acts by it. When he says he will do something, he does it. Nothing ever happens without his knowledge or consent and he is never taken off guard by some surprising outcome. As the old song goes, 'He's got the whole world in his hands' – and we are included. It makes you feel very secure, doesn't it?

When we know that everything that happens is guided by God, we can trust him in all sorts of puzzling circumstances. From a human point of view, much of God's will is mysterious. We question, 'Why did he allow that dreadful thing to happen?' But in the final analysis, we bow before a mind which is infinitely greater than ours and we remind ourselves that God declares:

As the heavens are higher than the earth, so are my ways higher than your ways and my thoughts than your thoughts (Isaiah 55:9).

God has a will for us

'If only I'd had a better upbringing.' 'I wish I'd never done that.' 'Why did God allow this to happen to me?' It is so easy to live on regrets and to believe that if our circumstances were different we would be of greater use to God.

We so quickly forget that God's will for us does not start now – it began before we were born.

• Consider Psalm 139:16.

God decided that he wanted you on the earth. He put you in a family and knew exactly what would happen to you. He saw your failures and successes, pains and pleasures. He drew you to himself and now, as your loving heavenly Father, he wants to continue – rather than begin – the plans he has for you.

• Correct the following statement:

For we are God's workmanship, created in Christ Jesus to do good works, which God prepared for us when we became Christians (Ephesians 2:10).

You are not useless to God, because God does not create useless things. If you feel that God will not use you because of something you have done, remember that Moses savagely murdered an Egyptian, that Peter fervently denied Jesus and that Paul brutally persecuted believers. If they had thought, 'God won't use me,' where would the church be today? God knows your weaknesses, but he still wants you to fit into the plan that he has worked out for your life since the beginning of time.

God wants us to know his will

Since God has a will for us, it stands to reason that we must be able to discover what it is.

- Consider what Paul says in Ephesians 5:17.

God does not expect us to wander around aimlessly, guessing at his plans for us. Rather, he wants us to be filled with the knowledge of his will. This does not mean that, to satisfy our curiosity, we ask him to map out our whole life in minute detail. It means, instead, that we receive from him the general drift of our life's calling and our function in the church. Paul said:

We have different gifts, according to the grace given us (Romans 12:6).

When Jesus stood up in the synagogue in Nazareth at the beginning of his ministry, he said that the Spirit had anointed him to preach and heal (Luke 4:18,19). He knew his role, even though he may have been unaware of his exact itinerary.

When the early Christians were faced with a food distribution problem, the Twelve said:

It would not be right for us to neglect the ministry of the word of God in order to wait on tables (Acts 6:2).

We ... will give our attention to prayer and the ministry of the word (Acts 6:4).

Clearly, the Twelve knew their area of service and did not want to allow other matters, however important, to encroach on God's will for their lives. Like Jesus, they needed no precise timetable. An awareness of God's general plan for them was sufficient to propel them into the streets to share the gospel. We read that Epaphras wrestled in prayer for the Colossians.

- What was his prayer for them? (Colossians 4:12)

If Epaphras prayed this prayer, he knew that God could answer it. Every one of us can be confident that we are following God's will for our life.

God wants us to do his will

When he became king, Saul was humble and wise – a person apparently keen to do God's will. Sadly, he did not live up to expectations. He disobeyed God who rejected him as king and looked round for a replacement (1 Samuel 15:26–28). David was anointed king in Saul's place and God said of him:

I have found David son of Jesse a man after my own heart; he will do everything I want him to do (Acts 13:22).

Before David died he 'served God's purpose in his own generation' (Acts 13:36). Jesus said, 'Whoever serves me must follow me; and where I am, my servant also will be' (John 12:26). Jesus wants us to be working alongside him, fulfilling his plan for our generation. He does not want us to cast backward glances at times of blessing in the past and assume that he will work in the same way today. We set our sails to the Spirit – only then will God's government be established on the earth.

On one occasion, a woman in the crowd called out to Jesus, 'Blessed is the mother who gave you birth and nursed you' (Luke 11:27).

- How did Jesus reply to her?

Only those who do the will of the Father will enter the kingdom of heaven (Matthew 7:21). Adam failed to enter because he was intent on doing his own will. The root of sinfulness is not, as many people think, failure to obey a list of rules. It is living your own way – and your way is not good enough.

Not only did Jesus constantly tell us that we should do the will of God, he gave us an example to follow.

- Read John 6:38.

- What did Jesus not want to do?

• What did he want to do instead?

In this instance, Jesus was speaking to crowds of people and was at the height of his popularity. Later, alone in the Garden of Gethsemane and facing a horrible death, he repeated to his Father his commitment. It is easy to say, 'I'll do God's will,' when the going is good. It is a mark of maturity to stand by your word when your world is falling apart around you.

What happened to Jesus appeared to be out of his hands. Pilate surrendered him 'to their [the people's] will' (Luke 23:25). So was he simply being carried along by circumstances?

• Read Isaiah 53:10 to find out.

Jesus knew that he had to die for the sins of the world. It was God's predestined purpose. Many other individuals in the Bible did not know God's plan until they looked back. Joseph was sold into slavery by his brothers but later he said to them:

God sent me ahead of you to preserve for you a remnant on earth and to save your lives by a great deliverance (Genesis 45:7).

Jesus said to his Father, 'I have brought you glory on earth by completing the work you gave me to do' (John 17:4). And on the cross he cried, 'It is finished' (John 19:30). We were born to accomplish the Father's will, to do the work that he has always had in mind for us. As we commit ourselves to God's plan for our lives, we will experience a deep sense of wellbeing and God will be glorified through us.

God wants us to enjoy doing his will

Some Christians are under the impression that God's will is 'important, burdensome and necessary'. Doubtless they have never read Romans 12:2 which says that God's will is 'good, pleasing and perfect'! God does not want to lumber his servants with a load of daily chores to plough through. He wants to give his sons something to do with their lives that they were made for and will actually enjoy.

- What does David say about God's will in Psalm 40:8?

Eve did not believe that God's will was good enough, so she tried to improve on it. Jesus, on the other hand, refused to snatch what was his. Instead, he willingly submitted to God's plan for his life because he believed that it could not be bettered. God's will was his 'food' (John 4:34) and that food could never be more satisfying. We are exhorted to 'test and approve' God's will (Romans 12:2). The only way to find out if his will is good, pleasing and perfect is to devote ourselves to it.

On occasions, God's will may be difficult to discern, even when we are living close to him. Abram faced this problem when he and Lot had to part company. Should he take the land on the left or on the right? It did not matter. God had already given it all to him. Sometimes what we choose to do is almost immaterial. Of greater interest to God is that we should be 'sanctified' (1 Thessalonians 4:3).

When we find ourselves in puzzling and even unwelcome situations, we are not necessarily to assume that we are out of God's will. God deliberately withdrew from Hezekiah in order to 'test him and to know everything that was in his heart' (2 Chronicles 32:31). And Paul and Silas were beaten and thrown into prison because they were acting for God and not because of disobedience to him (Acts 16:16–40). It is not God's will that we should complain about our circumstances.

- According to 1 Thessalonians 5:16–18, how should we respond to them?

Sometimes it seems that God is ignorant of people's sins! In fact, not only does he appear not to notice their wrongs, but actually blesses them in spite of what they are doing! Few things can be more frustrating for the Christian who is seeking God with all his heart! But in the final analysis, no one gets away with sin.

Do not be deceived: God cannot be mocked. A man reaps what he sows (Galatians 6:7).

- Read 1 Peter 2:15.

- How should we respond to people who speak foolishly?

The Bible says:

It is God who works in you to will and to act according to his good purpose (Philippians 2:13).

You are called not only to 'do the will of God from your heart' (Ephesians 6:6) but invited to enjoy doing it. Jesus was anointed with 'the oil of joy' (Hebrews 1:9). No one could have lived a happier life than he did – and he wants you to share his experience.

Surely the greatest satisfaction at the end of life is to look back and affirm:

I have fought the good fight, I have finished the race, I have kept the faith. Now there is in store for me the crown of righteousness, which the Lord, the righteous Judge, will award to me on that day (2 Timothy 4:7,8).

- Over the next week, review God's will for your life and ask him to make clear to you:

  His general plan for you.

  The role he would like you to have in the church.